Seared Productions in association with Theatre503
presents the World Premiere of

YEARS OF SUNLIGHT
By Michael McLean

Years of Sunlight had its world premiere
on 25 January 2017 at Theatre503

CAST

Bob John Biggins
Emlyn Bryan Dick
Hazel Miranda Foster
Paul Mark Rice-Oxley

CREATIVE & PRODUCTION TEAM

Writer Michael McLean
Director Amelia Sears
Set and Costume Designer Polly Sullivan
Associate Designer Elliott Squire
Lighting Designer Joshua Pharo
Sound Designer Elena Peña
Associate Sound Designer Richard Bell
Costume Supervisor Melanie Brookes
Assistant Director Natalie Denton
Dramaturg Dan Coleman

Stage Manager Rike Berg
Production Manager Nic Donithorn
Carpenter Ben Lee
Scenic Artist Ellie Pitt
Press and Public Relations Kate Morley PR
Publicity Photograph Stephen McCoy
Photography Alex Harvey-Brown
Trailer Kula Studios
Producer Alex Waldmann
Associate Producers Robyn Bennett & Anna Haigh

Special Thanks to
Jerwood Space, the Nursery Theatre, Stephen McCoy, Nina Steiger,
Shaun Evans, Colin Tierney, Dearbhla Molloy, Ian Redford,
Soho Theatre, the Young Vic, Royal Court, Emma Hayworth,
Francesca Moody, Eilise McNicholas, Judie Waldmann, Roy McCarthy,
Jon Tozzi, Alexandra Moloney and Sasha Yevtushenko

CAST

JOHN BIGGINS (BOB)

John's recent theatre work includes *Husbands and Sons* (National Theatre and Manchester Royal Exchange), and *Port* (National Theatre); both directed by Marianne Elliot. Other theatre credits include Neville in *Neville's Island* (Hull Truck); as well as appearances at the Dukes in Lancaster, York Theatre Royal, Derby Playhouse, Gateway Theatre Chester, Theatre Royal Plymouth, Clwyd Theatr Cymru, Sherman Theatre, Cardiff, The New Vic, Stoke on Trent, The Court Theatre Chicago and The Shaw Theatre in London.

Recent television credits have included *Drifters, Not Like This, Like That, Life's Too Short, White Heat, Law and Order* and as Jack Dee's irritating neighbour Clive in four series of *Lead Balloon*. Other TV credits include *Coronation Street*, Channel Five sitcoms *Respectable* and *Suburban Shootout*; two series of *Treflan* (S4C); *Blessed, The Thick of It, The Armando Iannucci Shows, My Dad's The Prime Minister* (BBC); *Man Stroke Woman* (Channel Four) and *Murder In Suburbia* (ITV). Other screen credits include *The Bill* (six times); *Casualty, Murder City, The Vice, Wall of Silence, Extremely Dangerous, Heartbeat, London's Burning, The Stretch, As Time Goes By, Duck Patrol, Adam's Family Tree* (three series); *The Knock, Expert Witness, Second Thoughts, The Sound of Stillness, EastEnders, Hope and Glory, Home Farm Twins, Pineapple Chunks, City Central, Breakfast Serials, Night Shift, There's a Viking In My Bed, Snow, The Final Passage* and *Two Pints of Lager and a Packet of Crisps*.

On film, John appeared in Lewis Gilbert's *Before You Go.*

In 2010, John spent six months with the BBC Radio Drama *Repertory Company*, and appeared in four series of the sitcom *North By Northamptonshire*.

BRYAN DICK (EMLYN)

For theatre his credits include *Hobson's Choice* (Theatre Royal Bath/ Vaudeville West End); *Seminar* (Hampstead Theatre); *Sliding With Suzanne*, *Plasticine* and *Bone* (Royal Court Theatre); *Lear* and *Amadeus* (Crucible Theatre); *The Life of Galileo* and *The Alchemist* (National Theatre); *Tinderbox* (Bush Theatre) and *Kursk* and *Public Enemy* (Young Vic).

For television his credits include *Capital*, *Wolf Hall*, *Bleak House*, *All the Small Things*, *Twenty Thousand Streets Under the Sky*, *Being Human*, *Shameless*, *Ashes to Ashes* and *Eric and Ernie*; and for film, *Colour Me Kubrick*, *Master and Commander*, *Brothers of the Head*, *Blood and Chocolate*, *Day of the Flowers*, *I Anna* and *The Numbers Station*.

MIRANDA FOSTER (HAZEL)

For theatre her credits include *Hamlet*, *Romeo and Juliet*, *God of Soho* and *The Bible* (Shakespeare's Globe); *Springs Eternal*, *The Marrying of Ann Leete*, *King Cromwell* and *Greenwash* (Orange Tree Theatre); God of Carnage (Nuffield Southampton); *The Talented Mr Ripley* (Royal and Derngate Northampton); *Madagscar* and *Shadow Language* (Theatre503); Shraddha (Soho Theatre); *The Lucky Ones* (Hampstead Theatre); *Pera Palas* (Gate Theatre); *Love You Too* (Bush Theatre); *The Criminals* (Lyric Hammersmith); *The People Downstairs* (Young Vic); *Blithe Spirit* (Manchester Royal Exchange); *Our Country's Good* and *A Doll's House* (Leicester Haymarket); *The Cherry Orchard* (Aldwych Theatre); *Gilgamesh*, *Schism in England*, *King Lear*, *Antony and Cleopatra*, *Neaptide*, *The Futurists*, *Pravda*, *The Government Inspector*, *Animal Farm*, *The Spanish Trajedy* and *The Fawn* (National Theatre).

For television her credits include *The Trial of Gemma Lang*, *Rosemary and Thyme*, *Dream Team*, *Where the Heart Is*, *Brotherly Love*, *Cockles* and *The Merry Wives of Windsor*.

MARK RICE-OXLEY (PAUL)

Theatre credits include *Poppy + George* (Watford Palace Theatre); *Playing with Grown Ups* (Brits Off Broadway); *Afraid of the Dark* (Charing Cross Theatre); *Tanzi Libre* (Southwark Playhouse); *Blood Brothers* (Phoenix Theatre, West End); *Town* (Royal and Derngate Theatres); *Switzerland* (High Tide Festival); *Much Ado About Nothing*, *The Merchant of Venice* and *Holding Fire* (Shakespeare's Globe Theatre); *Pool* (No Water); (Frantic Assembly); *The Romans in Britain* (Crucible Theatre); *The Life of Galileo* (Birmingham Rep Theatre); *David Copperfield* (West Yorkshire Playhouse); *Bright Phoenix*, *The Kindness of Strangers* and *The Entertainer* (Liverpool Everyman); *The Comedy of Errors* (Bristol Old Vic); *Cuckoos* (Barbican); *The Dwarfs* (Tricycle Theatre); *Workers Writes* (Royal Court Theatre) and *The Danny Crowe Show* (Bush Theatre).

Television credits include *Nigel Farage Gets His Life Back*, *Casualty*, *Whitechapel*, *Wpc 56*, *Doctors*, *Preston Passion*, *Land Girls*, *New Tricks*, *Hotel Babylon*, *Eastenders*, *Holby City*, *The Dwarfs*, *Mersey Beat*, *Judge John Deed*, *In Deep* and *Two Pints Of Lager and a Packet Of Crisps*.

Film credits include *The John Lennon Story*.

CREATIVE & PRODUCTION TEAM

MICHAEL MCLEAN (WRITER)

Michael started out as a member of the Liverpool Everyman Young Writers Group. He spent a year on the Paines Plough/Channel 4 Future Perfect Scheme and was a member of the Royal Court's Invitation group and selected for its "Supergroup".

Theatre includes *The Electric Hills* (Liverpool Everyman); *The Ducks* (Edinburgh Pleasance, Kellertheater Switzerland and Theater Stuhr Germany); *Grotesque Chaos* (Liverpool Playhouse Studio); *Athlete Agonistes* (Globe Theatre); *High Altitude* (Soho Upstairs) and *All Saints* (Trafalgar Studios 2).

Radio includes *The Tony Kay Scandal* (Radio 4).

TV includes *BBC New Comedy Awards* (BBC Three).

AMELIA SEARS (DIRECTOR)

Her previous work includes *The Last 5 Years* (Duchess Theatre); *Ant Street*, *Home* and *Brimstone & Treacle* (Arcola Theatre) and *Girls Guide to Saving the World* (HighTide Festival). She has worked as an associate and assistant at the National Theatre, West End, Donmar and Royal Court with Katie Mitchell, Michael Grandage, Jeremy Herrin, Joe Hill-Gibbins and David Hare and was also the recipient of the 2007/8 Bulldog Princep Directors' Bursary at the National Theatre Studio.

POLLY SULLIVAN (SET AND COSTUME DESIGNER)

Polly was awarded a first-class BA (hons) in Theatre Design at Wimbledon School of Art. Forthcoming work includes *Experience* (Hampstead Theatre, Downstairs); *Scarlett* (Hampstead Theatre/Theatr Clwyd) and *Educating Rita* (Queens Theatre).

Designs include *The Roundabout*, *Deny Deny Deny* (Park Theatre); *Firebird* (Trafalgar Studios); *Trouble In Mind*, *Forever Yours Mary-Lou*, *Monsieur Popular*, *The One That Got Away* (Ustinov, Theatre Royal Bath); *Matchbox Theatre* (Hampstead Theatre, Main Space); *Alligators*, *Pine*, *Firebird*, *Deposit*, *Elephants*, *Fault Lines*, *I Know How I Feel About Eve* (Hampstead Theatre, Downstairs); *The Snow Dragon* (St James Theatre); *Here*, *Donkeys' Years* (Rose Theatre, Kingston); *The Bomb – First Blast: Proliferation* (1940– 1992); *The Bomb – Second Blast: Present Dangers* (1992–2012); *The Riots*, *A Walk in the Woods*, *Tactical Questioning: Scenes From the Baha Mousa Inquiry*, *How Long Is Never:*

Darfur – a Response and Called to Account (Tricycle Theatre); *Flight Path* (Bush Theatre); *Hundreds and Thousands* (Soho Theatre); *Cotton Wool, The Atheist* (Theatre503); *Bear Stories* (Polka Theatre); *Aung San Suu Kyi – The Lady of Burma* (Riverside Studios) and *A Christmas Carol* (Chickenshed Theatre). As Associate Designer credits include *Les Misérables* (Wermland Opera, Sweden).

ELLIOTT SQUIRE (ASSOCIATE DESIGNER)

Elliott is a Canadian set and costume designer based in London. He is a graduate of Edinburgh's Scenehouse Programme, and also holds a Bachelor of Fine Arts degree in Theatre Design from the University of British Columbia. Select design credits include *The Marriage of Figaro* (Xi'an Concert Hall); *Shakespearean Rhapsody* (Carousel Theatre for Young People, Vancouver); *The Seagull* (UBC Theatre, Vancouver); and *Dirty Rotten Scoundrels* (Touchstone Theatre, Vancouver). As an Assistant Designer, his credits include *Peter Pan* (Chichester Festival Theatre); *A Room with a View* (Theatre Royal Bath); *First Light* (Chichester Festival Theatre) and *Running Wild* (Regent's Park Open Air Theatre).

www.elliottsquire.com

JOSHUA PHARO (LIGHTING DESIGNER)

Joshua works as a Lighting and Projection Designer across theatre, dance, opera, music, film & art installation.

Recent credits include *The Twits* (Curve Theatre, Leicester); *Removal Men* (The Yard Theatre); *Burning Doors* (Belarus free Theatre); *Broken Biscuits* (Paines Plough); *The Future* (Company Three); *Contractions* (Crucible Theatre); *Julie* (Northern Stage); *We're Stuck!* (China Plate); *Giving* (Hampstead Theatre); *Iphigenia Quartet, In The Night Time (Before The Sun Rises)*; *Medea* (Gate Theatre); *The Rolling Stone* (Orange Tree Theatre); *Glass Menagerie* (Nuffield Theatre, as Video Designer); *The Merchant of Venice, Wuthering Heights, Consensual* (Ambassadors Theatre); *Thye Crocodile* (Manchester International Festival); *One Arm* (Southwark Playhouse); *The Trial Parallel, A Streetcar Named Desire* (Young Vic); *Amadis De Gaulle* (Bloomsbury Theatre); *Beckett Season* (Old Red Lion); *The Deluge* (UK Tour, Lila Dance); *Usagi Yojimbo* (Southwark Playhouse); *Pioneer* (UK Tour, Curious Directive); *I'd Rather Goya Robbed Me of my Sleep, No Place Like Home* (The Gate) and *Thumbelina* (UK Tour, Dancing Brick).

www.joshuapharo.com

ELENA PEÑA (SOUND DESIGNER)

Theatre credits include *Layla's Room*, *The Muddy Choir*, *What The Thunder Said*, *The Littlest Quirky* (Theatre Centre); *Sleepless* (Shoreditch Town Hall, Analogue Theatre, Staatstheater Mainz); *The Man Who Would Be King* (Dawn State Theatre); *I Call My Brothers*, *The Iphigenia Quartet*, *Unbroken* (Gate Theatre); *Patrias* (Sadlers Wells Theatre, Paco Peña Flamenco Company, EIF); *We're Stuck* (One Tenth Human, Shoreditch Town Hall); *Ant Street*, *Brimstone And Treacle*, *Knives in Hens* (Arcola Theatre); *ISLANDS* (Summer Hall, Edinburgh, Bush Theatre & Tour); *For The Little People* (Caroline Horton); *THE CHRISTIANS* (Gate Theatre, Traverse Theatre); *Brainstorm* (ICT, National Theatre & Park Theatre); *You Have Been Upgraded* (Unlimited, Science Museum); *Storylab*, *The Kilburn Passion*, *Arabian Nights* (Tricycle Theatre); *Macbeth Digital* (Hightide, WAC & Tour); *Better Than Life* (Coney); *The Wardrobe* (Tricycle Theatre, NT Connections); *Girls Guide to Saving the World* (Hightide Festival); *Not Now Bernard* (Unicorn Theatre); *Macbeth Bwhb* (China Plate, WAC & Tour); *Sue The 2nd Coming* (Soho Theatre, Bristol Old Vic); *Pim & Theo* (Odsherred Teater, Denmark, NIE); *The Planet & Stuff* (Polka Theatre): *Flashes* (Young Vic); *Cooking Ghosts* (Beady Eye Theatre); *Mass Observation* (Almeida Theatre); *Quimeras* (Peacock Theatre); *Polar Molar* (MacRobert Arts Centre); *The Village Social* (National Theatre Wales); *Bette & Joan: The Final Curtain* (Foursight); *Quimeras* (Edinburgh International Festival); *The 13 Midnight Challenges of Angelus Diablo* (RSC); *Facebox* (National Theatre of Scotland); *gambling* (Soho Theatre); *Aspidistras* (Edinburgh Festival); *My Name is Sue* (Edinburgh Festival, Soho Theatre and UK tour); *Under Milk Wood* (Northampton Royal); *Plasticine* (Southwark Playhouse); *Punch & Judy Redux* (Dissentertainment, Edinburgh Fest) and *Fish Story* (People Can Run, Edinburgh Festival).

Sound Installation credits include *Have Your Circumstances Changed?* and *Yes These Eyes Are The Windows* (ArtAngel).

Television/Online credits include *Have Your Circumstances Changed?* (Online Films, ArtAnge); *Brainstorm* Live At Television Centre (BBC4 and iPlayer) and *The Astro Science Challenge* (Online Television Episodes, Unlimited Theatre).

Radio credits include *Duchamps Urinal* (Recordist/SD/Editor, BBC R4); *The Meet Cute* (Recordist /SD/Editor/Musician, BBC R4) and *Twelve Years* (Recordist / SD / Editor, BBC R4).

Elena is an Associate Artist for Inspector Sands where her credits include *The Lounge* (Summer Hall, Edinburgh); *Rock Pool, Seochon Odyssey* (HiSeoul Fetsival, Korea); *A High Street Odyssey* (UK Tour); *Undiscovered*, *A Mini Mass Observation Project* (South Bank Centre); *A Life In 22 Minutes* (Pulse, Ipswich) and *Mass Observation* (EIF). http://elenapena.co.uk/

RICHARD BELL (ASSOCIATE SOUND DESIGNER)

Theatre as Associate Sound Designer includes *The Children* (Royal Court); *Peter Pan Goes Wrong* (Mischief Theatre); *Blue Heart* (Orange Tree Theatre); *1984* (Headlong/Nottingham Playhouse/Almeida Theatre/Sonia Friedman Productions); *I Call My Brothers*, *Diary of a Madman*, *The Iphigenia Quartet* (Gate Theatre); *The Sugar-Coated Bullets of the Bourgeoisie* (Arcola/HighTide); *A High Street Odyssey* (Inspector Sands); *Henry IV* (Outreach Project for Donmar Warehouse).

Theatre as Sound Designer includes *Birthday Suit* (Old Red Lion Theatre/Pluck Productions); *Further. Still*, *Nailhouse* (Old Red Lion Theatre); *Wet Bread* (Sheer Drop).

Other media as Sound Designer include *Zombies* and *Run! Season 1&2* (Six to Start, Android/iPhone app).

MELANIE BROOKES (COSTUME SUPERVISOR)

Melanie studied a Fashion Design BA in Liverpool and then gained a MA in Fashion Design in Milan, Italy before starting a career in theatre and film. For several years Melanie has been costume supervising, costume making and working in wardrobe departments, including several West End shows, The Royal Opera House and Shakespeare's Globe. More recently, she been designing costumes and set for theatre and film.

NATALIE DENTON (ASSISTANT DIRECTOR)

Natalie graduated from Mountview Academy of Theatre Arts with an MA in Theatre Directing and is Artistic Director and co-founder of In The Attic Productions.

Directing credits include: *Fingertips* (C Venues, Edinburgh Fringe Festival); *All In The Same Boat* (Oxford House Theatre); *Spiritualists* (Rose Playhouse) and *At First Sight* (Karamel Club). Assistant Directing credits include the world premiere of *Teddy* (Southwark Playhouse) and *13* (Unicorn Theatre). She has also participated in the Rapid Write Response at Theatre 503 and a new writing showcase with Drift Theatre.

RIKE BERG (STAGE MANAGER)

Rike graduated from the Bauhaus University Weimar in Germany and has worked on various theatre productions in Sweden and the UK. Her most recent credits as Stage Manager/Assistant Stage Manager include *The Woman in Black* (Gothenburg English Studio Theatre and Sweden Tour); *Belongings* (GEST); *Upper Cut* (Southwark Playhouse); *Sense of an Ending* (Theatre503); *Lines* (The Yard Theatre); *Clickbait*, *Four Play*, *We Wait In Joyful Hope* (all Theatre503); *Fury* (Soho Theatre); and *Burning Bridges* (Theatre503). Since moving to London Rike has also worked for the Royal Albert Hall, Pleasance London, the Gate Theatre, the Bush Theatre and the Young Vic.

SEARED PRODUCTIONS (PRODUCER)

Seared is the creation of actor Alex Waldmann (RSC, Globe, National Theatre, Donmar Warehouse, Almeida, Cheek by Jowl). Founded in 2010, Seared is an independent theatre production company dedicated to the development and facilitation of work that is provocative, politically conscious, and, above all, entertaining. Previous productions include sell-out revivals of *Home* by David Storey and *Brimstone and Treacle* by Dennis Potter (Arcola); and premières of *Rose* by Hywel John, *The Ducks* by Michael McLean and *Pedestrian* by Tom Wainwright (Edinburgh Fringe Festival).
www.searedproductions.co.uk and @SearedProds

ROBYN BENNETT (ASSOCIATE PRODUCER)

Robyn trained at Theatre503 where she undertook an assistant producer residency. She is currently a freelance theatre producer and also assistant producer at Tara Finney Productions. Producing credits include *Dr Angelus* (Finborough Theatre); *The State We're In*, *BU21:RWR* (Theatre503) and *On The Line* (Merge Festival 2016).

As Associate Producer *Screens* (Theatre503) and *Your Ever Loving* (Theatre N16). As assistant at Theatre503 credits include *Clickbait*, *Four Play*, *BU21*, *Portia, Jelly Beans*, *We Wait In Joyful Hope*, *The Games We Played*, *Grey Man* and *Screwed*.

As assistant at Tara Finney Productions credits include *The Acedian Pirates* (Theatre503); *MUTED* (The Bunker) and *good dog* (Watford Palace Theatre & National Tour).

Robyn is a shortlisted producer for the Old Vic 12, 2016.

ANNA HAIGH (ASSOCIATE PRODUCER)

Anna Haigh Productions is an independent theatre production and general management company. In 2016 Anna produced *Last Of The Boys* (Southwark Playhouse) and *This Will End Badly* (Southwark Playhouse, and also produced *Ginger Is The New Black* at Edinburgh Fringe Festival 2016. In 2015 Anna was associate producer for *The Titanic Orchestra* (Pleasance Edinburgh). In 2015 AHP general managed *Smooth Faced Gentlemen* (Pleasance & Underbelly Edinburgh) and *James Hamilton Is So Lonely* (Voodoo Rooms Edinburgh).

Anna Haigh's previous work includes her alternate company Stormy Teacup Theatre Ltd, a theatrical company nurturing new musical theatre, which produced the Edinburgh Fringe hit of 2013 & 2014 as well as the hit UK tour *I Need A Doctor: The Whosical*. In 2013-2014 Anna completed her producer apprenticeship with Stage One at Seabright Productions Ltd. and Bill Kenwright Ltd.

Anna Haigh Productions has been generously supported by the Stage One Bursary Scheme. For more information, please visit www.stageoneuk.com

OUR SUPPORTERS

We are incredibly grateful to the following who have supported us, without whom our work would not be possible

The Harold Hyman Wingate Foundation, The Schroder Charity Trust, The Boris Karloff Foundation, The Idelwild Trust, Cockayne Grants for the Arts, The Peter Wolff Trust, The Sylvia Waddilove Foundation, The Thistle Trust, The Unity Theatre Trust, The Williams Trust, The Audience Club, M&G Investments, Barbara Broccoli, Wandsworth Council, Arts Council England Grants for the Arts, all our Friends and Point of Sale Donors.

We are currently in receipt of funding from Arts Council England's Catalyst Evolve fund – allowing us to grow our fundraising capacity by match funding income from new donors over the next three years.

Particular thanks to the Richard Carne Trust for it's generous support of our Playwriting Award and 503 Five

SUPPORT THEATRE503

In the last year alone, plays which started in our 63-seat studio have had: three West End transfers, two national tours, won or been nominated for 21 awards, and played to over 3800 people. We have staged the work of 106 playwrights since the start of 2015. We receive no regular core funding and we fundraise for all our in-house productions and creative development programmes.

Can you help us keep this going to nurture the next generation of theatrical talent?

If so, and you donate to us today we can match it.

We have been successful in securing funding from Arts Council England's Catalyst: Evolve project. This means that for every pound we raise from new donors, they will match that sum over the next three years. **So your gift of £20 becomes £40 (£45 with Gift Aid).**

You can make a donation online at www.theatre503.com/support/make-a-donation.

You can also text **DRAM16 £5, £10** or **£25** to **70070** right now.

If you would like to discuss supporting our new season or for more information about our work please contact Andrew Shepherd at andrew@theatre503.com or call him on 020 7978 7040

THANK YOU

GET INVOLVED

FRONT OF HOUSE

Our front of house volunteers get to see all our shows for free – and to bring a friend. Many get involved because of their passion for theatre, or because they live nearby, and many are also interested in developing their own practise. If you'd like to find out more please email volunteer@theatre503.com

RAPID WRITE RESPONSE

Theatre503 offers writers, directors and actors the chance to work together on our Rapid Write Response program. For every four-week show, we host a Writers' Night, which offers writers the chance to meet the literary team, and see the current show. **Writers** then have four days to write a ten-minute response piece inspired by the play that they have just seen. The best pieces are selected by the literary department to be staged two weeks later in our Rapid Write Response performances.

Interested in writing for RWR? Sign up to our writer's mailing list theatre503.com/sign-up/

Are you a **director** up for the challenge of casting and directing a short play in less than a fortnight? If so, please email rap@theatre503.com to find out more.

And for **actors:** can you rehearse, learn your lines and perform a new piece of writing in a matter of days? If so, we'd love to hear from you: please email rap@theatre503.com and explain how you'd like to be involved.

Not only is RWR a great way to get creative juices flowing, it's an amazing opportunity to meet other artists and develop creative relationships so do get in touch if you're interested.

YEARS OF SUNLIGHT

Michael McLean

YEARS OF SUNLIGHT

OBERON BOOKS
LONDON

WWW.OBERONBOOKS.COM

First published in 2017 by Oberon Books Ltd
521 Caledonian Road, London N7 9RH
Tel: +44 (0) 20 7607 3637 / Fax: +44 (0) 20 7607 3629
e-mail: info@oberonbooks.com
www.oberonbooks.com

A catalogue record for this book is available from the British
Library.

PB ISBN: 9781786821133
E ISBN: 9781786821140

Cover photograph by Stephen McCoy from series
'Skelmersdale 1984'

Printed and bound by 4edge Limited, Essex, UK.
eBook conversion by CPI Group (UK) Ltd, Croydon, CR0 4YY.

Visit www.oberonbooks.com to read more about all our books
and to buy them. You will also find features, author interviews and
news of any author events, and you can sign up for e-newsletters
so that you're always first to hear about our new releases.

*Thank you to Leo Butler, Dan Coleman, Roy McCarthy
and Amelia Sears for their help in writing this play.
Thanks also to the cast and everyone at Seared and Theatre503.*

Characters

HAZEL
Female, white, Irish accent, born 1950s

PAUL
Male, white, Liverpudlian accent, born 1970s

BOB
Male, white, Lancashire accent, born 1940s

EMLYN
Male, white, Liverpudlian accent, born 1970s

SCENE ONE – 2009

HAZEL   You're so still
      Standing out here all alone like a statue
      Surprised a dog hasn't piddled on ya

PAUL   Where are the dogs

HAZEL   What dogs

PAUL   All of them
      Next door
      The collie

HAZEL   Jesus Paul
      That thing died
      Don't know when
      Ten years
      Twenty years ago

PAUL   No

HAZEL   You were still here
      Sure you were

PAUL   Paddy

HAZEL   That's right
      Tatty thing
      Rubbed your legs
      They're all well gone son
      The dad died
      Empty now
      Some druggies time to time
      Then no-one
      I got you a drink
      I thought maybe
      We could drink
      To
      You drink red still don't you

> I know you're driving
> So I got you a mini bottle
> From the ninety-nine p shop

PAUL   How much was it

HAZEL   Ninety-nine p
Good one
Have you been up the stairs
Son
Up the dancers
Poked around

PAUL   Of course not
I hope you haven't been upstairs
What if it collapses

HAZEL   I stand in that living room and I have to close my eyes
Our poor little house
The times we've had

PAUL   I saw him

HAZEL   Who

PAUL   Emlyn

HAZEL   When

PAUL   Yesterday
Police let me
Drove all night
After you rang

HAZEL   You drove from Ireland

PAUL   Yeah

HAZEL   And you didn't come and see me

PAUL   You weren't here

HAZEL   They've put me in a guest house

PAUL   Yeah
        Some woman told me
        Some woman over in Bob's house

HAZEL   Oh
        Her

PAUL   Who is she

HAZEL   Some woman

PAUL   Related to Bob

HAZEL   No

PAUL   So where's Bob live

HAZEL   Bob's dead son

PAUL   Bob
        Since when

HAZEL   Since he died last year

PAUL   I didn't know that
        Did I

HAZEL   I don't suppose you did Paul
        Bob died in his bed
        A year ago
        And now some woman lives there
        With her
        Kids

PAUL   Well she saw me climbin
        The wall there
        The back door was open

HAZEL   You went in

PAUL   Yeah

HAZEL   And stayed over

PAUL   No
            No
            I just
            Stood
            Inside
            With the torch on me phone
            Everythin was just
            Black
            And then I
            Drove round the estate
            Slept in the car

HAZEL   You're crazy Paul
            If I'd have known you were here
            Have you got a nice car

PAUL   Yeah

HAZEL   What is it

PAUL   A Saab

HAZEL   What colour is it
            Did you see his face

PAUL   There wasn't one
            He had no face
            He was burnt to a crisp
            He was just a shape
            I couldn't
            The copper said
            When they carried him out
            He was black and charred
            Froth in his mouth
            There wasn't one

HAZEL   Does he get a
            A wake

PAUL   I don't know

HAZEL   Who'd know

PAUL   I don't know
I don't know

HAZEL   We could ring

PAUL   Yeah we could
Or maybe
We could just
Leave it
Leave it now
I've seen him
Off
Said our

HAZEL   That funny little face

PAUL   We need to get out of here
Mum
Have you got what you need from inside

HAZEL   Now

PAUL   We can't stay
There's nothin to stay for

HAZEL   Of course there is
This is our home
We've wine to have
Just
I only wanted to see him right Paul
I'd feed him
I let him stay when he had
I don't know
People after him

PAUL   What people

HAZEL   Not after him
He'd think things
He was just Emlyn

PAUL   I just assumed he'd disappeared
Off the face of the earth

HAZEL   Well he didn't
He hadn't Paul
People don't do that

PAUL   You shouldn't have

HAZEL   What
What

PAUL   Soft
Soft touch

HAZEL   And you're a fine one to tell me that

PAUL   What

HAZEL   You can't even process
If dogs or people are alive or dead
Even if it's just in your mind's eye
Or in flesh and blood
I'd known him since he was this high
Only he wasn't this high any more
He was this high
Brittle as a bird and not one bad bone
If I saw him I saw you
That's all there was to it
You're between the devil and the deep blue sea

PAUL   Ice cream

HAZEL   What

PAUL   Here's the ice cream van

HAZEL   I can't hear it

PAUL   I can

HAZEL   You always could hear it first
He'll make a killing in this weather

PAUL   I'll get us one
I'll go and catch him
Does he still stop in the U

HAZEL   Yeah
I'll get them

PAUL   Have you got money

HAZEL   Let me get you one
You wait here
It's a beautiful day

PAUL   There's not one spot
Of sun
In this yard
There never was
Any time of the day

HAZEL   No
The other side of the road's like the Copacabana

PAUL   He was born with them
Bad bones

HAZEL   For Christ's sake
You sound like a nun
I'll get us an ice cream

SCENE TWO – 2003

BOB   Oi
Oi

EMLYN   All right

BOB   Doon

EMLYN What

BOB   Ya doon

EMLYN What am I doin
       The gate's locked
       I'm lookin for someone

BOB   Eh down

EMLYN What

BOB   Down a there

EMLYN Get down
       I am gettin down

BOB   Down

EMLYN I'm gettin down aren't I
       There
       Happy now
       Oh
       It's you

BOB   Uhh
       Geh

EMLYN What you lookin at
       Where's Hazel

BOB   Na

EMLYN Is she on the bowlin green

BOB   Uh arr uh

EMLYN What you speakin like that for
       Were you dropped on your head when you were
       a baby or somethin

BOB   Uh

EMLYN Don't you recognise me

Do you know what planet you're on
You're Bob
I'm Emlyn
You live over on Hollowgreen
You used to work in the printers
You haven't got any kids
You used to drink Manns
You were always playin golf
You were into all that swingy showtuney shit music
Sinatra
Frank Sinatra
He's dead isn't he
Like you will be soon

BOB   Uh

EMLYN What
What are you gonna do
Look at the fuckin kip a ya
It's a bit of a
Leveller
Isn't it
Old man

BOB   Uh

EMLYN Where's Hazel
Try and stop me
Why don't you just point

HAZEL Bob

BOB   Uh

HAZEL Who you talking to Bob

BOB   Uh a there

HAZEL Oh
        Good God

EMLYN Hazel
        How are you

HAZEL Yeah
        Yeah I'm grand Emlyn
        What the hell are you doing here

EMLYN Nothin
        I thought you'd be here
        I knocked at yours
        And then I asked down the shop
        Said you might be here

HAZEL Yeah
        I am

BOB   Uh

HAZEL Yeah yeah it's fine Bob
        You go on back

BOB   Uh

HAZEL Honestly
        Get back to your game
        Go on
        Bob's not
        Had the best of times lately
        His wife's gone and so

EMLYN Really
        Ah
        You know I always picture Bob
        Just standin there
        With a bottle of Manns in his hand

HAZEL Do you now
        Where are you living Emlyn

EMLYN   Ah just you know
             Here and there

HAZEL   I don't have a clue if you're alive or dead or in peril
             and you swan up now

EMLYN   I'm alive
             Hazel
             I'm here I'm sound

HAZEL   What's that on your neck

EMLYN   What

HAZEL   Your neck

EMLYN   Oh nothin just
             I need to keep it covered
             I got an infection

HAZEL   What from

EMLYN   What

HAZEL   How did you get it

EMLYN   I dunno it just
             You know what my skin can get like

HAZEL   That looks so sore though

EMLYN   Nah

HAZEL   It's all yellow son
             On the bottom there
             The tape

EMLYN   That's just
             I've had creams
             It's fine
             How's your Paul

HAZEL   He's alive too I imagine

EMLYN   Hasn't he

HAZEL   No
        I try calling him I think maybe I've got the digits
        wrong the code the Ireland
        I'm sure he's grand I'm sure I'll hear
        In time

EMLYN   Course you will

HAZEL   I have to get back now
        Bob
        He needs his pills
        Jesus you look a state Emlyn

EMLYN   I don't do I

HAZEL   It looks septic

EMLYN   It's not septic it's just

HAZEL   Did someone attack you

EMLYN   No
        Ow

HAZEL   Is it off a rope or
        Is it a rope burn Emlyn
        You're all chafed round the other side too
        I mean come on Emlyn
        Let me see your wrists

EMLYN   What fuckin ell

HAZEL   And mind your tongue please

EMLYN   I meant bloody ell
        Sorry look just

HAZEL   What are you taking

EMLYN   When

HAZEL Now
If you tell me nothing Emlyn

EMLYN Nothin

HAZEL God almighty

EMLYN Nothin Hazel just the little caps just the methadone

HAZEL You take it everyday do you

EMLYN Yeah
Yeah never miss

HAZEL So what happened there then
Have you tried to do yourself in there Emlyn
Like some right eejit

EMLYN No
Hazel
Why would I do that

HAZEL Because you can tell me
Because if you've got
Bad thoughts or bad people after you all these years

EMLYN I got it with Bosh

HAZEL Bosh
You're still in touch with that little horror

EMLYN No he's all right now
He's in Liverpool
He's straight
He's got daughters and that

HAZEL Then why's he attacking you

EMLYN No he didn't
It's from a glider

HAZEL A glider

EMLYN I went handglidin
Bosh took me up
He flies it every Sunday from Formby beach
He's got these earpiece set things
For radioin in to the bases and all that
Only he doesn't use it for that
He puts his music through it
And he gets a bit stoned like
And so he takes off and flies over Bootle and Seaforth
stoned out of his head
Lookin down on all the houses and the roads
And he listens to a bit of Floyd
Can you imagine
What he normally does is
He gets up there and puts Dark Side of the Moon on
And when the last song finishes
He lands on the beach
And gets his missus to pick him up in the car
And he goes home and he has a roast

HAZEL Well
The less time you spend with men like that

EMLYN Yeah
I'm sorry Hazel
Do you want me to go

HAZEL Go where

EMLYN I just better
Leave you to it
You must be

HAZEL Must be what

EMLYN Embarrassed

HAZEL At what

EMLYN   I understand
        People lookin

HAZEL   They're waiting for me
        That's all

EMLYN   Yeah
        I'll go
        What are you playin
        Triples

HAZEL   Singles

EMLYN   Winnin

HAZEL   Losing

EMLYN   Oh well
        Keep goin eh

HAZEL   Yeah
        My hands are all bent and all
        Ready for the knackers yard

EMLYN   Where's your bracelet
        Still got it

HAZEL   Course I have
        It's back home
        It's in the house

EMLYN   Yeah

HAZEL   It's empty
        It's an empty house now
        Your room there's just
        Still there

EMLYN   Paul's room

HAZEL   Paul's room
        Emlyn

Look at me
When's the last time you ate some hot food

EMLYN Doesn't matter

HAZEL Tell me
Emlyn

EMLYN God knows

SCENE THREE – 1998

PAUL How does it glow

EMLYN Snap it

PAUL Won't it all come out

EMLYN No
They're leak proof
Just snap it

PAUL In the middle

EMLYN Yeah that's it
Go on
Be brave
There
That's it
Now shake it

PAUL Is that it

EMLYN Give it a wave
Bright yellow
Not bad eh

PAUL How long's it last

EMLYN Bout twelve hours
Sometimes longer
Specially when it's this cold

PAUL   How much do I owe ya

EMLYN   No mate
You have it
On the house

PAUL   Come on
How much

EMLYN   It's fine Paul
Happy new year

PAUL   How much do you sell them for

EMLYN   Three for a fiver
Got necklaces and bracelets too
Mostly kids want them tonight

PAUL   Where'd you get them

EMLYN   I work for someone
He imports them
He's in Wrexham tonight
They're mad for them down there
Do you know what they do
They split the casin and get the liquid out
And rub it straight onto their faces and neck
and hands and arms
So they all glow in the dark
Can you believe that

PAUL   Yeah I can
So what else does he sell then
This bloke

EMLYN   What do you mean

PAUL   Bit of a front is it
For other stuff

EMLYN   No
Just glow stuff
Does all right
Not tonight though
It's deadly

PAUL   It's baltic

EMLYN   Yeah
Feet are like ice
I knew it was you you know
When you walked up
From a distance
From the dock
Way you walk
Hasn't changed
I thought
I don't believe it
It's Paul
In a big coat
Dressed all smart
Did you know it was me

PAUL   When

EMLYN   When you passed me

PAUL   Didn't see ya
That's why I passed ya

EMLYN   I thought you looked at me

PAUL   I didn't see ya

EMLYN   I couldn't shout your name at first
Must've been the cold
It's great to see you mate
You live in Dublin still then yeah

PAUL   Yeah

EMLYN   Don't they have a big New Year party

PAUL   Yeah
They have a big fight
Big massive city fight

EMLYN   Are you er
Are you pissed are ya mate

PAUL   Dunno
Am I

EMLYN   Well
You do look a bit merry

PAUL   Good
Money well spent then

EMLYN   Yeah
You on your own are ya

PAUL   Tonight
Or in life

EMLYN   Tonight

PAUL   Yeah
On my own

EMLYN   Not married or that are ya

PAUL   Why wouldn't I be

EMLYN   No just
I dunno
You might be

PAUL   Yeah I might be
I might have ten kids by now

EMLYN   Yeah
So are ya
With someone
Or that

PAUL   I've walked out

EMLYN Right
         Sorry Paul
         These things happen eh
         Are you movin back over here then

PAUL   No
         I work there
         I live there now

EMLYN Forever
         You think

PAUL   Yeah

EMLYN What is it you do
         It's computery isn't it

PAUL   Yeah
         Computery
         How about you
         Four bedrooms and a garden is it
         Big Volvo
         Wife called Debbie

EMLYN Yeah
         No
         I'm in Wrexham

PAUL   With the glow baron

EMLYN Just
         Stay with people there yeah

PAUL   Doin what

EMLYN Just you know

PAUL   No
         What

EMLYN Just
Bits like this

PAUL So
No paintin then
No artwork

EMLYN Er
No
Wish you know
I could
But it's sort of
Impossible

PAUL Is it

EMLYN Yeah

PAUL Why

EMLYN Just is
Hard
It's startin to snow
Look

PAUL Any bogs round here

EMLYN Not sure

PAUL Where've you been goin

EMLYN I haven't really needed
What you doin

PAUL I can piss in the sea can't I

EMLYN Right
There's a few people walkin up you know
Paul
They've got kids with them

PAUL   Fuck it
        I don't know how you put up with it you know

EMLYN   With what

PAUL   Bein a fuckin tramp
        Bein on the street all the time and bein frozen
        stiff and havin nowhere to piss or shit or get warm
        or do anythin

EMLYN   I'm not a tramp

PAUL   No
        Well
        It's unbearable anyway

EMLYN   I just
        I've just got a blanket while it's a bit
        There y'are look it's gone
        You have it

PAUL   I don't wannit
        I'm goin

EMLYN   Where you stayin
        Are you stayin in your mum's

PAUL   No

EMLYN   Oh
        How is she
        Has she had a nice Christmas

PAUL   Dunno ant spoke to her

EMLYN   Why not
        She's only up the road

PAUL   Because I don't wannoo

EMLYN   Oh right
        Just thought

If you're spendin new year in Liverpool
then you must have been over to Skem too

PAUL   Well I haven't

EMLYN   Why've you come to Liverpool then

PAUL   Because
         Maybe I wanted to
         For new year
         Try it
         See what the city's like now

EMLYN   And what do you think

PAUL   All I can find are braindead bars
         Endless shit chrome bars with shit shit music
         Mouthy shitehawks off their faces
         It's hard to join in
         Isn't it

EMLYN   You should see your mum mate

PAUL   I do see her

EMLYN   Not often

PAUL   How the fuck would you know

EMLYN   Just
         She misses ya
         She'll be missin you now
         She's only up the road

PAUL   Well why don't you go and see her then
         She thinks the world of you doesn't she

EMLYN   I might
         I plan to
         It's been a while

PAUL   Has it now

EMLYN Yeah

PAUL Since what
Since she loaned ya

EMLYN No
You should see your mum

PAUL Do you see yours

EMLYN What

PAUL Do you see your mum

EMLYN Dunno what you mean
Not very nice is it

PAUL What

EMLYN If I had a mum maybe I would

PAUL Course you've got a mum
Everyone's got a mum
Everyone comes from somewhere

EMLYN Not everyone knows where their mum is
You don't know who your dad is

PAUL Yeah I do
It'll just be some thick fuckin mick who couldn't bear
her for longer than five minutes
I don't blame him
And I don't blame her for gettin outta there either
Irish people are as annoyin as they look you know
They'd fuckin love you

EMLYN You don't mean that
About your mum
She was always there

PAUL All right then
Your foster woman
What was her name

EMLYN June

PAUL June
Do you still keep in touch with her

EMLYN No

PAUL Why not

EMLYN She moved away
When I first moved out

PAUL Exactly
You moved away
She moved away
People move away
Don't they

EMLYN Sometimes

PAUL I was gonna be a dad

EMLYN When

PAUL In the new year

EMLYN And
Now you're not

PAUL I've walked out

EMLYN Right
Can't you walk back in

PAUL Have you got any money

EMLYN What

PAUL How much money you got
I'm stayin in a hotel
Up the road
I haven't got cash on me
I've got some in the room

EMLYN Oh right
       Yeah

PAUL   I'm burstin here
       I just need a piss and a sit down and some heat

EMLYN Yeah I've got cash
       Sold a fair bit tonight

PAUL   Does he pay you Emlyn
       He doesn't take you completely for a ride does he
       This bloke
       I mean you do take a cut don't ya

EMLYN Course
       This is my work
       He'll box me off tomorrow back in Wrexham

PAUL   How you gettin down there
       There'll be no trains or buses tomorrow you know

EMLYN No I know I'll just
       I can walk it

PAUL   What

EMLYN I can walk it

PAUL   You can walk to Wrexham

EMLYN Yeah
       It's not that bad

PAUL   Not that bad
       It's not even in this country
       There's about three rivers in the way

EMLYN It's not it's fine
       You can go via Runcorn
       If you go through Runcorn way it takes
       Half a day

PAUL   You got that money ready then
           I'll flag a cab

EMLYN   Here y'are
           I'll pay
           Where's the hotel

PAUL   Top end

EMLYN   Got a fiver here
           Or tenner
           New Year innit

PAUL   Yeah go ead
           Give us that
           Keep an eye out for a cab

EMLYN   There y'are you keep hold of the money mate

PAUL   Listen
           All I can say is
           Be careful
           In life and also doin all this
           Walkin to Wales

EMLYN   Ah don't worry about me
           I'll go in the mornin

PAUL   Take care

EMLYN   Yeah sound mate but
           Not sayin bye yet are we

PAUL   Yeah
           I'm goin the hotel

EMLYN   I know but
           You want me to come with ya yeah

PAUL   Thought you were workin

EMLYN   I am but I'm done now
        It's gone midnight

PAUL   Oh right

EMLYN   So shall I come back with ya

PAUL   Er
        Well
        Not really no

EMLYN   Oh
        No

PAUL   I'm stayin in a hotel

EMLYN   I know
        I could come back with ya like
        Chance to

PAUL   What

EMLYN   Catch up

PAUL   We just have

EMLYN   Yeah but I mean
        Properly
        Can't I come back with ya
        Have a drink maybe

PAUL   I've finished drinkin
        I've finished Emlyn

EMLYN   Oh

PAUL   That's the difference
        You and me
        I know when to stop

EMLYN   I meant maybe a cuppa

PAUL   Yeah
        A cuppa

Then somethin else then somethin else
We're adults
Emlyn
I'm an adult

EMLYN   Right
        Okay
        Tarra then Paul
        Maybe
        Another time
        Or you know
        You never know
        Do ya

PAUL   No

EMLYN   Bye mate
        Paul
        Do you remember
        First drink we had together
        Cherry brandy
        On the prom
        In Rhyl
        Paul

PAUL   Wine

EMLYN   What

PAUL   It was cherry wine

EMLYN   God
        First sip
        I can taste it
        I can feel it
        I can feel the sun burnin down
        Paul

PAUL   What

EMLYN What's it gonna be
       Girl or boy

PAUL   Boy

SCENE FOUR – 1993

HAZEL You know he died and went to heaven the other week

PAUL   Emlyn

HAZEL He woke up underneath the stars
       And he convinced himself he'd passed over
       He was on a roundabout
       By the motorway
       Him and Bosh had swallowed a bag of trips
       or God knows
       Anyway he's on his back
       And all he can see is the night sky
       A full moon
       Clear as anything
       And bright white stars
       And he looks left and right and the roundabout's so big
       And the grass and trees are whispering
       He thinks he's dead
       He sits up and he can still see lights and people and life
       But no sound and just a soft breeze
       And so he thinks "I better tell them"
       And so he knocks on a house
       And this fella answers
       And Emlyn says
       Sorry to trouble you mate
       The thing is I'm actually dead
       I've just died about an hour ago
       And I need to ring
       I dunno the council or police or someone
       And this fella says "You what mate"

And Emlyn says "I'm dead mate
Can I use your phone"
God bless us
Can you imagine

PAUL   What did the fella do

HAZEL   Well he did some damage
He got hold of a baseball bat or summat
And knocked him unconscious all over again
I saw him outside the shops
He didn't look good

HAZEL   Look at him now though
The proper little artist
The shapes
The colours
He's got some talent hasn't he
Can we buy one

PAUL   Which one

HAZEL   Any
One for our house
And one for your new place
Could you take one over do you think

PAUL   Course I could

HAZEL   Big canvas on your wall
To look at when you get in at night
Your mate's work
Here he is
Vincent Van Gogh
With two ears
Look at you both there
Pinky and Perky
He's very proud of his mate aren't you Paul
To be here for his big night

EMLYN Thank you for comin
Thanks Paul

PAUL My pleasure
Congratulations

EMLYN Yous had any wine

HAZEL We have
It's gone straight to my head

PAUL Have you

EMLYN Nah

HAZEL Have a glass

PAUL He doesn't want one

HAZEL Who was that taking your picture
She looks very proud of you
Kisses and all sorts

EMLYN Ah just the council woman
She sorts it all for me
Gets me the studio
Lets me have it whenever I want
Sometimes I sleep there
I paint through the night
Finish as the sun comes up

PAUL They shouldn't let you sleep there

HAZEL He's an artist

PAUL Yeah and he's a
Man too
They need to support him

HAZEL They do

EMLYN I like the small hours anyway
It's the best time

PAUL   To what

EMLYN Capture
        What I'm tryin
        To paint

PAUL   Which is what

EMLYN Just
        Whatever it is
        I don't know what it is
        It's broken things
        The cracks
        The colours
        Man made
        All of them
        They're the colour of somethin that's gone
        Some things just
        Linger
        Don't they
        And if you try hard enough you can bring them back
        If you get some flattened red paint
        Sort of like the top of your wine
        If you flatten that and wash and pour and roll
        it goes pinky on the edges
        That was our colour
        That council red was what all the seats
        Benches
        Bus stop colours
        Were painted
        The council painted all the front doors didn't they
        Or you could choose your colour
        So not all the front doors were the same
        Yours was light blue

HAZEL That's right

EMLYN   But you still had those sort of red drain pipes
        It was a bit sort of
        Aston Villa

HAZEL   That's right
        I can see it
        It's all been painted over now mind

EMLYN   Yeah
        Well
        I can see
        The old
        The pipes
        The benches
        The lamp posts
        The bus stops
        The things that were made out of metal and wood
        All the years of sunlight would turn them into
        somethin else
        They weren't pressed out of coloured plastic
        Which is what you get now
        You get all those Fisher Price bus stops now don't you
        Where everythin's luminous
        Injection
        Dyed
        It's not the same is it
        There isn't some fella comin out
        Paintin every couple of years
        Puttin the colour back
        They just
        Take it all away

PAUL   Yeah

EMLYN   Yeah so
        There you go

PAUL   I want one

EMLYN   A picture

PAUL   Yeah

EMLYN   Which one

PAUL   I'm gonna pick one

EMLYN   Yeah

HAZEL   What if I want the same

PAUL   You'll have to fight me for it won't ya

EMLYN   You really want one

PAUL   Of course mate

HAZEL   Paul
        Get me a top up

PAUL   Right

HAZEL   Well
        You've really done us proud Emlyn

EMLYN   Thank you for comin
        Made up you brought him

HAZEL   He wouldn't have missed it
        He's come back over specially I reckon

EMLYN   You think

HAZEL   And then as we walked up
        Saw the board outside
        His eyes lit up
        His eyes welled up

EMLYN   No

HAZEL   Yeah

EMLYN   Pity no-one's here

HAZEL   Well that's to be expected

It's raining out there

EMLYN   I know
         But
         They said
         If I sold a picture or two
         They might even give me
         A grant
         Money to live off

HAZEL   You take it son

EMLYN   Yeah
         But Hazel
         First thing I'd do

HAZEL   What

EMLYN   Give it to you

HAZEL   Give what to me

EMLYN   The cash

HAZEL   Don't be ridiculous
         For what

EMLYN   All the times

HAZEL   What

EMLYN   I've taken
         From you

HAZEL   Shush now
         Forget the past
         The future's yours son
         Grab it
         Forget the past

EMLYN   How can I

HAZEL   What's done is done

Now you've done this
And these people here
Have helped you
Paul doesn't know what he's saying sometimes
he just gets

EMLYN I know
But he's puttin his faith in me I have to repay it don't I

HAZEL What

EMLYN His faith his help
He's gonna help me

HAZEL By buying a painting

EMLYN No
By takin me

PAUL Here
Chin chin
To Emlyn

EMLYN Thank you

PAUL You need to go and get a sticker mum

HAZEL A sticker

PAUL Yeah

HAZEL For what

PAUL You pick a picture
And put a sticker on
To reserve it
Go on
I'll pay don't worry
I'll write a cheque at the end
Go
Well mate
This is it

EMLYN   Yeah

PAUL   It's all startin to work itself out
        They'll love you you know
        The Irish

EMLYN   Yeah

PAUL   Ah mate
        You wouldn't believe it
        Emlyn

EMLYN   Yeah

PAUL   Yeah
        Now you know what you need to do

EMLYN   What's that

PAUL   Tell the truth

EMLYN   What truth

PAUL   When you talk to them
        When you talk about your art
        When we're over there

EMLYN   Right
        What's the truth

PAUL   Your truth

EMLYN   What's my truth

PAUL   Everythin you've done
        Everythin you've gone through to become this
        Painter
        Artist

EMLYN   It's not very positive though is it

PAUL   Who wants positive

EMLYN   I do

PAUL   That's not art though is it
        The ugly stuff is art
        Guilt is art
        You can capture it
        It'll help you move on

EMLYN   What I'm tryin to create
        Doesn't bring up guilt
        It's innocence
        Isn't it

PAUL   But you're not

EMLYN   Not what

PAUL   Innocent
        When your childhood involves sniffin varnish
        before you've even begun to shave
        Innocence is gone

EMLYN   I didn't always do that
        There was a time you know
        Before that

PAUL   When
        There wasn't though
        Was there
        Not for you
        It's not your fault
        You're still here aren't ya
        So now you can go somewhere else
        And create somethin new
        Somewhere else

EMLYN   What if I don't want somewhere else

PAUL   Why wouldn't you

EMLYN   Because
        There was a time

> There was
> And a place
> Here
> That I can get
> Again

PAUL   You won't ever get that back
Emlyn
You've got another chance
Haven't ya
I'm givin you another chance
But listen
I'm not messin
I mean it
Next week

EMLYN   I don't know what to say Paul

PAUL   We can go over to Ireland
Next week
Leave here for good

EMLYN   Yeah
I er
Next week

HAZEL   I've picked
I've picked my one
Emlyn

PAUL   You see
It's a decision
Isn't it mate
Emlyn

EMLYN   Yeah

PAUL   Next week
No vanishin acts
No disappearin off the face of the earth

HAZEL   Why
        Where are you taking him

PAUL   He's comin with me
        You're comin with me
        Emlyn
        To live

HAZEL   To live

PAUL   Yeah

HAZEL   But he's on
        Courses
        Schemes and he's got his medicines all in order

PAUL   I'll sort it
        I'll sort all that it's all bullshit anyway it's all failed
        hasn't it
        Look
        He agreed
        We agreed
        You agreed
        Didn't you
        Emlyn

EMLYN   Yeah

PAUL   It's a decision

HAZEL   Then let him make it

PAUL   He's made it
        He's already made it
        You'll be spendin your time
        Free
        Emlyn
        Walkin by the river
        Clearin your head
        Listenin to some albums with me again

> Sleepin in a bed of your own
> Rentin your own studio
> I'll get you a studio
> A huge room
> For free

HAZEL Free

PAUL You wouldn't believe
It's the opposite of here
There's money and life and ideas and culture
and people

HAZEL I don't see how you can be so sure of that Paul

PAUL It's where I'm from

HAZEL Well your voice tells me you come from round here
You don't know a soul over there
You've no family there
Your only family's me
Mine's only here when you visit
And now you want to take him away too

PAUL Well if you had any sense you'd be away from here
and you'd come back over too

HAZEL You don't know what you're talking about
I was told something similar when I left that country
Just get myself over here
With you
And I'd be sure to find what you're promising him now

PAUL Look
He's already decided
Emlyn

EMLYN Yeah

PAUL   You've already decided
       Haven't ya
       Emlyn

EMLYN Yeah

SCENE FIVE – 1988

EMLYN Sleep
       That's it
       Wave your hands
       Come on higher
       Superman
       Hitch a ride
       Okay
       Now sneeze
       Achoo
       Say it
       Achoo

HAZEL Achoo

EMLYN Go for a walk

HAZEL God bless us
       That's probably enough now Emlyn
       I get it
       Switch it off now maybe

EMLYN See I can do all the actions
       Honest Hazel this'll be me if this happens
       Startin now
       And then up and up and up

HAZEL That's just it
       I don't want you up and up
       You're always up

EMLYN You always said I'll be a millionaire

HAZEL I did

EMLYN So that's what I'm gonna do

HAZEL You're going to be a club disc jockey

EMLYN Yeah
       Just
       I have to pay
       The man
       Hire his gear
       Two speakers one amp one mixer
       I'll buy me own eventually
       Once I'm earnin
       Just need this start
       You're not convinced are ya
       But I actually just
       I thought you
       Of all people

HAZEL Me what

EMLYN I thought you'd be fuckin
       Yes yes go go

HAZEL You're not speaking properly son
       What have you taken
       Do you want some dinner

EMLYN I don't need dinner
       I just need a quick lend
       To pay this guy

HAZEL I don't have cash to be giving out son
       You know that Emlyn

EMLYN I know that's what I'm sayin
       It'll get paid back when I get paid and then I'll pay
       you more
       Please Hazel

Thirty quid tops
Or twenty

BOB   Hazel
Hazel

EMLYN   Fuckin ell

HAZEL   Oh it's Bob
Over here

BOB   Everythin okay

EMLYN   Why wouldn't it be

BOB   Who the fuck asked you
Where've you been Hazel

HAZEL   I've er
I've been out to get Paul new shirts
He's got his practical exams

BOB   Well see him
He's been here all afternoon

HAZEL   Been where

BOB   Round ere
Loiterin

HAZEL   Let's all stay calm

EMLYN   Litterin
I haven't dropped any litter

BOB   Loiterin
Loiter

EMLYN   Sorry
It's your accent

HAZEL   What do you mean loiterin

BOB   Hangin about

EMLYN It's too strong for me

BOB   What is

EMLYN I can't quite tune into the Lancashire accent

BOB   You're in Lancashire you cheeky little tramp

EMLYN Yeah but I don't speak it

BOB   No but you fuckin live here
       Thousands of ya

EMLYN We had no choice
       We were sent here from Liverpool

BOB   No and we had no choice either
       So why don't you fuck off back up the motorway
       And leave us lot in peace

EMLYN Do you wanna batman Bob

BOB   You what

EMLYN Do you wanna batman

BOB   Did someone drop you on your head when you were
       a baby

EMLYN No

BOB   Well they fuckin shoulda done
       What's your Paul doin even talkin to him
       I thought he'd moved on
       I thought he had exams

EMLYN Dunno if you noticed
       But I've been comin to this house since I was that high
       And I'm not that high any more
       I'm this high
       So maybe you should go away

BOB   You're fuckin high all right
       High as a kite
       I've seen you

EMLYN   Seen me where

BOB   On the golf course
        That's where
        You and all the rest of them
        And we're fed up
        That was a crackin peaceful golf course that
        You know summat Hazel
        You can't hit a decent drive on the fairway no more
        Cos by time you get to where the ball's landed
        Some arsehole's made off with it
        I mean how perverted is that

HAZEL   Come on now

BOB   I'm tellin you Hazel
        You don't wanna be lettin him in here
        You wanna get some locks on your gate
        I'll fit em for ya

HAZEL   We don't need any locks fitting thank you Bob

BOB   Me and us older lot
        We can see right through him
        And this new youth
        Juiced up to the hilt on fuckin
        Solvents
        And it's us who'll have to deal with it
        Cos even if your Paul ends up goin away to a Poly
        or settlin down
        This shitehawk'll still be buzzin around
        With sod all to do and sod all to his name
        Like this whole town
        A Liverpool smack colony

HAZEL   No-one's on smack here thank you

BOB   I told you it'd happen
        In this town

It'd come to fruition
It's like rivers of blood with Scousers
Let me tell you this
There was meant to be a dinner dance
In the clubhouse last Friday
And do you know what the volunteers
All ladies
What they found in the mornin when they opened up
A bloody smashed mess
With needles
And empty cans
And puke and piss and shit all over the carpet
I'm sorry Hazel but this needs sayin
And do you know
The biggest sickener
On the wall
We've a picture
In a frame
Of our patron
Raises thousands for spastic kiddies
Fuckin one of his lot in fact
Jimmy Tarbuck
Big colour photo of him we had
In a frame
And you know what someone had sprayed on
this picture
Big red words
FAT TORY CUNT
Yeah
Yeah
How about that
But there's more
Picture of the Queen
Above the bar
Been there since God knows

Know what they sprayed on that
Same
FAT TORY CUNT
About the Queen
The Queen
That's all you've got to know Hazel
About the likes of him
The likes of him who can do that
Can do anythin
Oh yeah
By the way
Lad
Frank Sinatra
Alive and well
Eh

EMLYN   You what

BOB   Frank
        Sinatra
        Alive and well

EMLYN   Eh

BOB   Frank Sinatra
        Alive
        And well

EMLYN   Speak English a minute

BOB   I am speakin English
        And I'm tellin you
        In no uncertain terms
        That Frank Sinatra's still alive
        So whatcha think of that

HAZEL   Bob

BOB   You hear what I said

EMLYN What

BOB   Frank Sinatra
Lookin great still
Soundin great
Isn't he

EMLYN Who's that

BOB   SINATRA
You know who he is
You know

EMLYN Who

BOB   Frank Sinatra

EMLYN Isn't he dead

BOB   No he fuckin well is not
He's alive and well and his music will be alive for
a long long time after you've croaked
Which I hope is very soon indeed
And I mean that most sincerely

EMLYN Nice one
I'm havin a batman
D'you want one

BOB   A what

EMLYN A batman
Orange and lemonade

BOB   You're not made right you
You know that

EMLYN D'you want one then

HAZEL Right come on now that's enough
Emlyn go and get some ice from the shed for your drink
Go on go

EMLYN   Tarra Bob

HAZEL   I'm sorry Bob

BOB   Don't apologise to me Haze
I'm just
Bewildered
Why a woman like you is mixed up with someone
like that

HAZEL   He's Paul's friend he's a good lad really he's

BOB   Hazel
Love
A good lad is what he is not
He's an addict
It's dangerous for a woman like you on your own
He's dangerous
He's only after one thing and that's to take
To steal
He'll turn
Nasty
I can see it's gettin to ya
Love
Hazel

PAUL   Mum

HAZEL   Paul love

BOB   Hello lad
I'm just
Checkin in
On your mum
Paul
He's here

PAUL   Who

BOB   Him

PAUL   Where

BOB   Out there

PAUL   And what

BOB   Paul
Do the right thing by yourself eh
You can do so much better lad
Than that
And ya mum
She can do so much better an all

EMLYN   Oh
You still here Bob

HAZEL   Wait
Bob

EMLYN   All right Paul

PAUL   Where you goin

HAZEL   To see him

EMLYN   She always goes after him

PAUL   How'd ya mean

EMLYN   Do you think his wife likes him comin round here
all hours

PAUL   What hours
He doesn't come round here

EMLYN   Not when you're here maybe
I've seen him though
You might wanna get a grip on your own house Paul
I'm havin a batman
You want one

PAUL   I'm all right thanks
You okay

EMLYN Yeah sound
       Been playin some tunes with your mum

PAUL   Right
       What ones

EMLYN Led Zep Sabbath Deep Purple Gong Beefheart
       Final Cut

PAUL   With me mum

EMLYN Only messin
       D'you wannoo though

PAUL   I can't
       Sorry mate

EMLYN Why not

PAUL   I've got a lot of work to do
       Where were you today

EMLYN Dunno

PAUL   I saw ya
       In the cemetery

EMLYN Oh

PAUL   From the science block
       We all saw ya
       The teacher gathered us round to look
       He was laughin his head off
       It was you and Bosh and all the others
       You had a gluebag in your hand
       And you were on top of the fence
       Emlyn

EMLYN Was I

PAUL   You were stuck
       On the railings

Like some kinda
Pigeon
Flappin away
Till you fell on ya head
All the class were pissin themselves
And you left your Sunblest bag on top and started
tryna knock it down with a stick

EMLYN Can't remember

PAUL   You know from the top of that science block
All you can see are these navy blue dots
Spread out
Lads and girls
Scurryin round in twos and threes
Completely wasted
Then lyin on the grass till it gets dark
Why'd you do it
Emlyn

EMLYN Here y'are
Take some of this

PAUL   What

EMLYN This
Ronson fluid
Have a bit
Suck it between your teeth

PAUL   Put it away
Put it in the bin
Emlyn

EMLYN I'm havin a drink

PAUL   Well finish it yeah but

EMLYN You know what Paul
I sometimes look at you

PAUL   And what

EMLYN   Can I borrow your record player

PAUL   Why

EMLYN   I've got a job

PAUL   Really
          Where

EMLYN   Playin records
          Down the club
          Do you want me to show ya

PAUL   I can't not now

EMLYN   Well you won't be needin this record player then eh

PAUL   I do need it
          Emlyn
          Put it down please

EMLYN   Why
          Why should you have it
          You didn't pay for it did ya

PAUL   What you talkin about
          It's mine
          It was a Christmas present

EMLYN   Did you pay for it

PAUL   What

EMLYN   Why should you get Christmas presents and not me

PAUL   Emlyn

EMLYN   Where's my Christmas presents
          Where's my fuckin family and fuckin things eh
          You stuck up prick

PAUL   Stop it

EMLYN   It's fuckin mine now
        You can go down the ock shop Monday if you want it
        back
        Cos I'm gettin some fuckin cash for it first

PAUL   No you're not
        Emlyn

EMLYN   Get the fuck away
        I'll fuckin chiv ya
        You and your fuckin mum

PAUL   Stop

EMLYN   Tell her to fuckin stick her batman
        Tell her to keep droppin her knickers for Bob
        To keep her sorted for odd jobs round the house
        To keep a man in her life
        Cos no other knobhead'll go near her
        I'm havin this
        I'm takin somethin back

PAUL   From who

EMLYN   From fuckin
        Anythin
        Give me some money for a bus
        In your pocket
        Move your arms
        Move them
        Paul I'm sorry but this is just the way it is
        Other pocket
        Paul
        Move your arms
        I'll fuckin snap them off you Paul I can't stop meself now

PAUL   You can

EMLYN   No
        I can't stop

I can't
How can I
How can I stop this

SCENE SIX – 1982

HAZEL   Just calm down
        The pair of you
        You're all het up
        Look at you
        Skinny malinks
        Like lobsters in that sun
        What have you eaten today

PAUL   We've had lolly ices

HAZEL   Well that's not much use is it

PAUL   We're on holiday

HAZEL   You still need to eat properly

EMLYN   Lager and lime ones we had
        And shandy

HAZEL   So you've had a skinful then
        Ale monsters

PAUL   It's not real alcohol

HAZEL   Have you saved me any treats then
        Could just have summat sweet

EMLYN   I've got a chewy
        Won it on the penny machine

HAZEL   The one in your mouth

EMLYN   No
        I won two

HAZEL   You keep it
        And don't swallow it

EMLYN   Why not

PAUL   Wraps round your heart

EMLYN   Does it

HAZEL   And clogs your arteries

EMLYN   Where are they

PAUL   In your bum

HAZEL   Er thank you

EMLYN   Oh yeah erm
        Hazel
        I erm
        Won this too for ya
        From the machine
        Was gonna save it till we leave but
        If you're dressin up tonight
        Goin out

HAZEL   Come on then what've you got me

EMLYN   I think it's a
        Er
        I dunno actually

HAZEL   It's a bracelet
        A charm bracelet

EMLYN   Is it

PAUL   Wally

HAZEL   Button it you
        Now Emlyn
        I think it's the nicest thing anyone's ever given me

Apart from the Toblerone I get from Paul every Christmas
Eh Paul
Would you look at that
It's wonderful
Thank you
Could you tie it up for me there
My fingers are like navvies'

EMLYN   Yeah
What do you do

HAZEL   There should be a catch there

EMLYN   Oh yeah
It's titchy
I er
I can't get it
Paul can you do it

PAUL   Here y'are
Here y'are let go a sec
It won't catch

EMLYN   There y'are it goes through there
Like a key ring

PAUL   Yeah but it should just

EMLYN   You got it

PAUL   Yeah

EMLYN   That's it

PAUL   Ang on a mo

EMLYN   Let go

PAUL   Yeah

EMLYN   Yeah
There y'are

HAZEL   Are we done

EMLYN   Done

HAZEL   Perfect
        It fits
        I shall wear it tonight with pride
        Okay

EMLYN   Yeah

HAZEL   That's set me up that has
        Saturday night eh boys
        Saturday night fever in Rhyl
        I'm heading down the club
        You don't mind do you
        Bingo and a band
        Chicken in a basket

EMLYN   What's that

HAZEL   It really is
        Chicken in a basket
        You eat it
        And then they clear the dancefloor for a disco

EMLYN   Really

HAZEL   Yep

EMLYN   Is it good

HAZEL   Can be
        Just you know
        The way these things tend to be

EMLYN   It sounds
        Excitin

Music from off. Ska.

HAZEL   Oh

I wouldn't have thought son
Not as exciting as lager and lime lollies and penny
machines

EMLYN I bet it is

HAZEL Well
I wish I was your age again
Ready for a night in me jambos
Top to toe in bed
With your games and your sweets and
Your dreams
Look at you both there
Pinky and Perky

EMLYN Thanks so much
You know
For lettin me come with you
And you Paul

PAUL Shurrup

HAZEL Well now
You're very welcome
Aren't you Emlyn
Isn't he Paul

PAUL Spose

HAZEL He's very fond of you you know
Emlyn
Paul is

PAUL God

HAZEL He said so
Straight away
Before I'd even met you
One day
After school

       Said he'd met someone
       Lad called Emlyn
       Boss runner
       Boss drawer
       Boss music
       I'll never forget

EMLYN Yeah

HAZEL Ah yeah
       So listen
       Tonight
       I've done you some suppery tea

EMLYN What's suppery tea

HAZEL Tell him Paul

PAUL   Half supper half tea

HAZEL Now there's pop
       White and strawberry
       Juice to make batmans
       Butties
       Cheese and tomato
       Cheese on its own
       Salmon paste
       Jam
       No butter on any
       There's Panyan and there's crackers
       Make your own
       Have an apple each please
       Plenty of Clubs
       But don't go overboard
       Wash your hands
       Wash your faces
       Teeth before bed
       Doors locked windows shut

Telly on till ten at the latest
Then sleep
Right gents

PAUL   I thought it was ten thirty

HAZEL   Was it ten thirty last night

EMLYN   Yeah

HAZEL   Ten thirty then
Up bright and early for breakfast
Then the bike ride

EMLYN   Are you gettin a bike Hazel

HAZEL   No

EMLYN   Why not

PAUL   She can't ride

HAZEL   I could ride you off the road John Willy
I'll just be holding your stuff and watching love
No more bikes for me now
Watching you have fun
That'll do for me
Watching my Paul
And watching you too Emlyn
Watching you grow
And grow
And grow
And grow

Music up a notch.

What's up with you two
You both look tranced

EMLYN   We both
Out there
We've had a drink

PAUL Shurrup

HAZEL A drink of what

EMLYN Alcohol

PAUL God

HAZEL You mean the lollies

EMLYN No
Drink

HAZEL I hope you're joking me

PAUL We haven't
We had a tiny sniff and a
Taste

HAZEL Where was this

PAUL By the sea

HAZEL And what are you doing sipping alcohol by the sea

EMLYN We saw a girl didn't we Paul

HAZEL Oh aye
What girl's this then

EMLYN Just out there before
She was older
There's loads of them
And she was
She was all in white

HAZEL Was she now

EMLYN Yeah
Yeah they all were
They were wearin like
What were they wearin Paul

PAUL Sort of like decoratin overalls

HAZEL   Nice

EMLYN   But she'd like sprayed them
           With glitter

PAUL   And purple paint

EMLYN   And her hair was purple too

PAUL   No it was blue

EMLYN   Was it

PAUL   Sky blue

EMLYN   Yeah
           In bunches but

PAUL   Shaved a bit

EMLYN   Yeah

HAZEL   Good God

EMLYN   But guess what the best bit was

HAZEL   You mean I haven't heard yet

PAUL   No

EMLYN   Her handbag
           Was a kettle

HAZEL   A what

EMLYN   A kettle
           A leccy one

HAZEL   A kettle

EMLYN   She had it over her arm
           Like that

PAUL   She had stuff in it

EMLYN   It was white

HAZEL   To go with her overalls

EMLYN   Yeah
          But
          Like
          She was
          She
          Stood out

HAZEL   She sounds it
          Was she pretty

EMLYN   Oh yeah
          Yeah
          I mean
          Out of this world

HAZEL   Did you talk to her

EMLYN   Not really

PAUL   A little bit

EMLYN   They all came up to us
          They said we were dead funny
          Cos we were so little
          And one of them said
          Taste that
          And Paul said no
          But I said yeah
          And I did
          I took a big swig
          And they were laughin
          And then they walked off
          But this girl
          She bent down to me
          Put her hand
          On the back of me neck
          I could smell her

She smelt like pear drops
And she was
Dead warm
And I felt this kiss
On my bonce
Above my eyes
Like just sort of above inbetween my eyes
And then she let go
And then she ran off towards the sea
To catch her mates

HAZEL   Good God
Well I hope you aren't gonna be sick now
What sort of drink was it

PAUL   It was red

HAZEL   Red what

EMLYN   It was called cherry brandy

PAUL   No it was cherry wine
She said

EMLYN   It was burny
Burny hot down the throat

HAZEL   Was it horrid

EMLYN   No

HAZEL   Bob
Here's Bob
I'm ready
Are you heading over now

BOB   Aye
She's down there gettin the seats with the others
I said I'd get you

HAZEL   Great
         I'm ready
         I'll get my bag
         I've got a half bottle
         Scotch for ya

BOB   Lovely
         She's got gin

HAZEL   I won't be a sec
         There's a bottla Manns there for ya

BOB   Don't mind if I do
         Night in eh boys

PAUL   Yeah

BOB   Got your pop

PAUL   Yeah

EMLYN   Batmans

BOB   What

EMLYN   We're havin batmans
         Orange juice and lemonade

BOB   Orange and lemonade eh
         Get you
         What's your name again

EMLYN   Emlyn

BOB   Emlyn
         And how old are you two now

PAUL   Nearly eleven

BOB   Nearly eleven eh
         Big lads

PAUL   Yeah

BOB   Adventure eh

PAUL   Yeah

BOB   Where's your mum and dad then son

EMLYN   Mine
Oh er
I live with
Other people

BOB   Other people
Who
Your Grannie

EMLYN   No
Just people
Guardian woman

BOB   Oh aye
A Banardos boy are ya

EMLYN   A what

BOB   Found in the woods

PAUL   He lives up Kestrel
With others
In a house
Gets looked after

BOB   Do you now
Kestrel eh
Up by my golf course that
I'll have to look out for ya
You're a strange little fucker aren't ya
You there's somethin about you
Int there
Not right
Tell you what

> Listen to that music
> Out there

PAUL   Do you like it

BOB   No I bloody do not
> Bloody headbangin
> No way
> I'll be dancin later
> Some proper sounds

EMLYN   How old are you then

BOB   Eh
> Me
> Key to the door lad
> Twenny one

PAUL   No you're not

BOB   Eh
> Tell you summat
> Fun I had
> As a young boy
> Golden days
> Me and my brothers
> You didn't mess with us
> Golden days
> Still smell em
> All the dancin
> All the music
> Proper music

BOB sings "Golden Days". One minute long.

Music up a notch.

What a voice
Mario Lanza
A tenor

Ant even heard of him have ya
Who'd you both listen to
Eh

PAUL   Rush and Zappa

BOB   You what
Russian Zapper
What the hell's a Russian Zapper
What about showtunes
What about Sinatra
Frank Sinatra
You ever listen to him
Eh
A man of respect
Sorry boys
Ant got a clue
Gone to pot has knowin how to be a youngen now
What's she doin in there
I'm soberin up here
Fuckin woman

EMLYN   We've just had a drink

BOB   Oh aye
Drink of what

PAUL   Cherry wine

BOB   Cherry wine
Where'd you get that stuff

EMLYN   Off some girl

BOB   That figures
Bloody poof's drink when you have it
This is a man's drink

PAUL   What is it

BOB   Manns
It's called Manns
You ever had any of this
You ever had Manns

EMLYN No

BOB   You will one day
You'll learn
Bloody cherry wine

EMLYN I won't

BOB   You what

EMLYN I won't

BOB   You won't what

EMLYN I won't ever drink that

BOB   Oh aye
Gonna be a good boy are ya
Teetotal

EMLYN No
I just know
I can tell you now
For a fact
When I grow up
I won't ever drink that
Never
Never ever
And I won't ever listen to that music you sing
Or play golf
Or wear glasses
And I won't ever ever look like you
I'll never ever look like you

BOB   That so

EMLYN Never
       Never ever ever

BOB   Ah
       I see

EMLYN I think he's dead by the way

BOB   Who is

EMLYN That singer you said

BOB   What singer

EMLYN Frank

BOB   Sinatra

EMLYN Yeah

BOB   Frank Sinatra

EMLYN Aye that's the one

BOB   Frank Sinatra's dead
       What you talkin about
       Dead since when

EMLYN Just saw it in the cafe
       On the news

BOB   What news
       I dint see no news with that on

EMLYN The telly news
       HTV

BOB   HTV
       Why the fuck would it be on HTV
       He lives in Vegas he dunt live in fuckin North Wales

EMLYN Dunno
       Just was
       He's dead
       Plane crash they reckon

BOB   Plane crash

EMLYN Into the sea
          Where all the big sharks swim
          They reckon
          Don't they Paul

PAUL   Dunno

BOB   Son
          Tell me somethin
          Do you think
          You're even remotely
          Funny
          Do you think
          You're even remotely
          Worthy
          Of talkin about a man
          Like that
          A star
          Who's got everythin
          When you
          Are not even fit
          To share the same oxygen
          As him

EMLYN Dunno

BOB   No
          Come here a second
          Let me see your face
          Give us a smile
          Go on
          Big smile
          Go on

EMLYN This is it

BOB   That your biggest smile

EMLYN Yeah
       This is it

BOB   That it

EMLYN It is

       BOB hits EMLYN. PAUL doesn't move. Ten seconds.

HAZEL Here we are
       We set then
       Everything okay
       Emlyn

BOB   I think he's sunstroked
       What's that on your wrist

HAZEL A bracelet

BOB   Who off

HAZEL Emlyn
       He bought me a present

BOB   A present
       Did you lad
       Isn't that good of ya
       What a nice thing to do for Hazel
       What's it made of

HAZEL It's pure white gold
       Isn't it
       He's a gentleman
       Aren't you sweetheart
       Right
       Okay then
       I'll see yous
       Okay Paul

PAUL   Yeah

HAZEL Tarra Emlyn

Son
Okay then

Music stops.

Ta ta
Be good boys

PAUL   Mate
Mate
You okay
Shall I grab our food
Emlyn

EMLYN Comin out

PAUL   What

EMLYN You comin out
Let's go out
Let's do somethin
Let's drink somethin
Come on

PAUL   No

EMLYN Come on
Let's do it
Come on
I'm goin
I'm goin out
I'm gettin out there
It's all happenin out there
Let's get involved
Stick your shoes on
Come on
I'm gettin out there

PAUL   Wait

EMLYN   You comin
        Come on

PAUL   Don't

EMLYN   What

PAUL   Don't
        Don't be daft
        Don't go out
        Stay in here
        With me
        Don't

EMLYN   Why not

PAUL   Just don't

EMLYN   Let's get out there

PAUL   Please
        Don't go out

EMLYN   I'm goin
        I'll see ya
        I'm gettin out there
        Gotta get out there
        I've got to
        I'm gone

SCENE SEVEN – 2009

HAZEL   Here
        Dreamer
        Ice cream

PAUL   Cheers

HAZEL   What a day for it
        You'd think you were in the desert
        Look at our house

PAUL   Yeah

HAZEL   I'd run you a bath
Days like these
You'd be playing all day
Twelve hours or more
You'd love a long bath
With the window open
And the music playing
Light summer nights

PAUL   Yeah

HAZEL   I'd go upstairs and the bathroom door'd be shut
A song playing
I'd stand outside and listen
And I'd hear your little splashes and it'd mean
the world to me
I'd listen for an age
You'd be listening to the hit parade
The top forty
The countdown
Every Sunday

PAUL   Yeah

HAZEL   So I'd wait for the song to end
And the man to start yapping
And that's when I'd flick the plug off in the hall
And you'd shout "What"
Hadn't even said anything
You'd just shout it
Automatic
And I'd say "You want some suppery tea"
And you'd say "Yes please"
And I'd say "You having a batman"
And you'd say "Yeah"
And I'd say "You washed your hair"

And you'd say "I will in a bit"
And I'd say "Wash the spuds out your ears"
And you'd say "Can't hear ya"
And I'd say "Good one"
And I'd switch the plug back on
And the song'd fade up
And you'd splash about
And I'd stand like a statue on the landing
That little square bit
Listening
For an age
I used to float down the stairs
There's a knot
Deep down
And it never goes away

PAUL   What was he doin
          His last night

HAZEL   He was very quiet
          I went to the club
          Left him to it
          Was still light
          Funny thing is
          He ate all his tea
          He could never finish a meal
          He'd fall asleep
          You'd see his head drooping after a mouthful or two
          Sometimes his head'd hit the plate
          Because he'd have taken something
          You know
          But this night
          He polished it off
          Mash
          Then I caught him
          In the hall

Bent over
He said he was squirtin out blood
He'd get so ill
He'd be squirtin out blood from every hole you could
think of
He said he felt like a baby
He looked like a
Prisoner
Of war
I just
Gave him the remote
Rubbed his arm
And then I went out
And he smoked you see
He smoked in bed when I was out

PAUL   It's a miracle to me

HAZEL   What is

PAUL   That he lasted that long
That he kept you
Spellbound
All that time
Into middle age
On a plate for him
You kept it on a plate for him

HAZEL   I saw him I saw you
So strike me down

PAUL   He was absolutely nothin like me
He would've killed you
I told you when I finally wrote him off
He'd finish you off
Rubbin his arm
Feedin him mash
As good as stickin it straight into his neck

HAZEL For Christ's sake
Am I not to be
Seen
Reprieved on some level
If I'm never to be thanked
Or God forbid understood
For refusing to banjax the poor little bastard
How can I do that
Why would I do that
There is no relief
It's a permanent misery
It can be nothing but torture for the boy
Existing like that

PAUL I gave him a chance
You fuckin ruined it

HAZEL How did I

PAUL I tried to take him with me
You wouldn't let him go

HAZEL That's ridiculous

PAUL You think a plate of hot food's more important
than changin your life

HAZEL I didn't stop him Paul that's ridiculous
He made his own decisions

PAUL You're a liar Mum

HAZEL Look
Look
Here
Paul
Look at this
I took a photo one night
Of him

    Here
    And I made him look at it the very next morning
    Look
    I made him look at it all the bloody time when he let
    himself down
    Look at it
    Look at him there

PAUL   Yeah
    I'm lookin

HAZEL   I keep it
    To show him

PAUL   He's dead

HAZEL   I know he is

PAUL   They're my teddies
    Mum
    They're my teddies by his arm there

HAZEL   He wouldn't touch them they're just
    I kept all your stuff neat he must've knocked them
    I promise

PAUL   No I'm not worried about my teddies
    Mum
    I'm not worried about some stupid teddies am I
    I'm just pointin out to you
    There's a man
    On the floor
    Dribblin
    Holdin a teddy
    And you let him live with you

HAZEL   I didn't let him live I just
    We tried our best
    I gave him a chance

You weren't here
I was
I got him jobs doing piece work in my place
But his fingers and thumbs were all swollen and black
and his mouth was so ulcerated he couldn't even ask
for somebody to help him he was trapped Paul
He'd ask us to lock him away for days
We fitted the door with padlocks
He even fitted them with Bob he was brilliant he
really wanted it but he couldn't live without it you
just can't
You didn't even live here Paul
You don't know the half of it

PAUL   It doesn't matter now
This is all finished now
Come on

HAZEL You're going

PAUL   We're goin

HAZEL Where to

PAUL   We need to go
We'll stay at the Hilton
Then we'll get the boat

HAZEL The Hilton

PAUL   Yeah
We'll stop at Liverpool
On the way

HAZEL To where

PAUL   Dublin
I've booked us
We can go now
Mum
You can go

HAZEL   I've things to
             See to

PAUL   Like what
             Mum
             There are no things

HAZEL   The Hilton hotel

PAUL   Yeah
             Mum

HAZEL   You know they put us in the very worst house

PAUL   When
             Last night

HAZEL   When you and I got here
             When you were a tiny baby
             It was the worst house
             The wrong one
             We were last off the bus
             I shoulda said something
             I was all on my own though
             You were fast asleep in my arms
             We had big beautiful house in the city
             When we first got to Liverpool
             My brother said you take that baby and you go
             and you give him love and you give him life
             And he bought me my ticket
             And I never looked back
             Your bedroom alone in Liverpool was bigger than I
             could have wished for
             And then we got the letters
             And they kicked us out
             And knocked our house down
             And shipped us here to the arse end of nowhere
             What could I do

Who were we to turn around
Who are we
I owe subs

PAUL   Subs

HAZEL   My club
I owe double from the last Tuesday club
Mrs Mac
You remember Mrs Mac

PAUL   Yeah I remember Mrs Mac
Shall we drive round now and see her

HAZEL   And what

PAUL   And pay her

HAZEL   And tell her what

PAUL   That
You're finished
You're leavin
Mum

HAZEL   And go where

PAUL   Ireland

HAZEL   And what's there
For me
Whose is the football

PAUL   What football

HAZEL   The flyaway football
And the little shorts
On the back seat of your car out there
Since when have you played football

PAUL   I don't I just
Kickabout
In the park

HAZEL   Who with

PAUL   We need to go
Mum
I'll tell you later
Come with me and I'll tell you
We need to go
We'll stop at Mrs Mac's
Come on
Mum

HAZEL   Did I ever tell you about the time he died and went
to heaven

PAUL   Yeah

HAZEL   He'd retell it and retell it
Underneath the stars
On his back
All he can see is the night sky
A full moon
Clear as anything
Looks left looks right
Grass and trees whispering
Thinks he's dead
Sits up and can still see lights
And people
And life
No sound
Just a breeze
He thought he was dead
Can you imagine

PAUL   Yeah
Yeah I can
Come on

HAZEL   What

PAUL   Are we set
Mum
We'll go now
We'll check in
And tomorrow we'll get the boat
Okay
Mum

HAZEL   I don't have a thing to my name anymore

PAUL   You don't need a thing

HAZEL   I don't have a passport

PAUL   You don't need one
We'll get the boat
Okay

HAZEL   This was our house
They put us here

PAUL   Yeah

HAZEL   This was our home
This was our new life
Who was I
How old is he
Your son

PAUL   Nearly eleven
Mum
Come on
That's it now
Mum

HAZEL   No
It's not

PAUL   It is
That's it
This is it

Come on
Come on let's go

END.